BBQ Bible Cookbook

3rd Edition

Over 50 Barbecue Recipes for Every Meathead & Grill Lover!

by Olivia Rogers

Copyright © 2017 By Olivia Rogers
All rights reserved. No part of this book may be reproduced in any form without permission in writing from the author. No part of this publication may be reproduced or transmitted in any form or by any means, mechanic, electronic, photocopying, recording, by any storage or retrieval system, or transmitted by email without the permission in writing from the author and publisher.
For information regarding permissions write to author at
Olivia@TheMenuAtHome.com
Reviewers may quote brief passages in review.

Please note that credit for the images used in this book go to the respective owners. You can view this at: TheMenuAtHome.com/image-list

Olivia Rogers
TheMenuAtHome.com

Table of Contents

Who is this book for? 6

What will this book teach you? 7

Introduction 8

1. Grilled Shrimp Skewers Over White Bean Salad 9

2. Classic Hamburger 11

3. Green Chili Bison Burger 13

4. Grilled Fish Tacos 15

5. Grilled Chicken with a Touch of Chili and Lime 17

6. Steak, Potato Kebabs and Cilantro Sauce 20

7. Moroccan Shrimp with Spinach 22

8. Grilled Steak Served with Fresh Corn Salad 24

9. Smoky Ham and Corn Salad 26

10. Grilled Steak with Pepper Relish 27

11. Mojito-Rubbed Chicken with Grilled Pineapple 29

12. Spiced Pork Tenderloins with Mango Salsa 31

13. Steak Sandwich with Grilled Onion 33

14. Juicy Rosemary Chicken Skewer Kabobs 35

15. Grilled Garlic and Pepper Steak with a Caprese Salad .. 37

16. Quick and Easy Italian Grilled Chicken 39

17. Paprika Shrimp with Lemon Aioli 41

18. Chicken Souvlaki with a Delicious Tzatziki Sauce 43

19. Sweet and Spicy Grilled Pork Tenderloin 45

20. Bacon Stuffed Zucchini Boats 47

21. Rosemary Stuffed, Bacon Wrapped Chicken 49

22. Sweet n Spicy Grilled Pineapple Rings _____ 51
23. Hamburgers Topped with Mushrooms and Swiss Cheese ___ 53
24. Tandoori Chicken Thighs _____ 55
25. Honey Flavored Grilled Shrimp _____ 57
26. Spicy Asian Pork Skewers _____ 59
27. Sweet and Savory Salmon on the Grill _____ 61
28. Delicious Black Bean Patties _____ 63
29. Honey Chicken and Vegetable Skewers _____ 65
30. Chicken Tikka Masala _____ 67
31. Tangy Grilled Chicken _____ 69
32. Stuffed Jalapenos Wrapped in Bacon _____ 71
33. Grilled Garlic and Pepper Shrimp _____ 73
34. Honey Garlic Steaks _____ 75
35. Butter Basil Shrimp _____ 77
36. London Broil _____ 79
37. Grilled Fish Tacos with A Zesty Lemon Dressing _____ 81
38. Butter Beer Chicken _____ 83
39. Fiery Shrimp _____ 85
40. Bacon Wrapped Hamburgers _____ 87
41. Grilled Zesty Tilapia with a Sweet and Spicy Mango Salsa __ 89
42. Orange and Garlic Grilled Tuna _____ 91
43. Sweet Pineapple Chicken Skewers _____ 93
44. Country-Style Pork Ribs _____ 95
45. Simple and Tender Prime Rib _____ 97
46. Gourmet Steak with All the Fixings _____ 99
47. BBQ Beef Ribs _____ 101

48. Steak Sandwich	*103*
49. Rib Steaks with a Fresh Salad	*104*
50. Olive and Cheese Burger	*106*
51. Sweet and Sour Grilled Steak and Peppers	*108*
52. Quesadillas with a Difference	*110*
53. Japanese-Style Grill	*112*
Conclusion	*115*
Final Words	*116*
Disclaimer	*118*

Who is this book for?

Grilling is a great way to prepare your food – it gives it a flavor second to none and is quick and easy.

In this book, we have rounded up the best grill and barbeque recipes we could find so that you never need to feel short on inspiration again.

Every recipe in this book has been tested and is finger-licking good. It's time to fire up the barbeque and invite some people over so that you can show off your skills as a master griller.

This book is for anyone who hates having to spend hours slaving over a hot stove. The recipes are tasty, fairly healthy and designed to be easy to prepare.

What will this book teach you?

You will learn how to grill or barbeque a range of different meats and vegetables so that you have maximum flavor for minimal effort. We have recipes to suit every palate – from our good, old-fashioned burgers to our fiery Green Chili Bison burgers.

You'll learn how to grill seafood, chicken, beef and pork so that it is done to perfection. You'll also learn a little more about some of the ingredients and have a perfect range of fun facts to show your friends that you are more than just a master griller.

We will even make it easier for you to let out your saucy side out with recipes for delicious sauces to accompany your meats. We have rounded up the very best recipes for you to enjoy.

Introduction

The recipes in this book are designed to cause a stir – everyone will be asking for seconds if you serve them and only you will know how little effort it took to prepare them.

We have basic crowd pleasers such as classic burgers and more exotic dishes like our Mojito-Rubbed Chicken with Grilled Pineapple. Fancy a spicy twist on old favorites? Try our Grilled Chicken with Chili and Lime.

Seafood lovers, we have not forgotten about you. Try the Grilled Shrimp Skewers with White Bean Salad or our Grilled Fish Tacos.

Every dish in this book was composed with the finest, freshest ingredients in mind. The recipes are bursting with flavor and nutrition and are sinfully delicious.

This is no diet cookbook – you get to enjoy delicious food without having to worry about the carb count, calorie count or number of grams of fat. All you have to worry about is enjoying your food.

And, when it comes to your summer barbeque or grill, that is all you really want to worry about anyway. So, let's get started so that you can dig in.

1. Grilled Shrimp Skewers Over White Bean Salad

The two main ingredients of this dish; the grilled shrimp and the white bean salad go hand in hand to create a heavenly flavor combination. Serve this dish as a starter or fire up enough to make a full meal out of. Soak the skewers in cold water for about an hour before putting them on the grill to prevent them getting too singed.

Ingredients

- 1/3 cup lemon juice
- 3 tablespoons olive oil
- 2 tablespoons fresh minced oregano
- 2 tablespoons fresh minced chives
- 24 peeled and deveined raw shrimps
- 12 cherry tomatoes
- 1 teaspoon ground pepper
- 1/2 teaspoon salt
- 30-ounce cannellini beans

Method

1. Mix the lemon juice, olive oil, chives, oregano, salt and pepper in a bowl. Add beans and tomatoes to the paste and toss well. Heat the grill to a medium high temperature to provide the optimum conditions.

2. Oil the skewers and stick the shrimps onto six of them and prepare them to be cooked. Make sure that you turn the skewers every four minutes so that the shrimps do not get burnt and they are cooked properly. Dress the shrimps in the end and serve them with the bean salad.

Did you know?

The lemon juice which has been used in this recipe has numerous advantages. The fact that it is slightly acidic in nature helps to break down the food in your stomach which aids in the effective and quick digestion.

2. Classic Hamburger

Who doesn't love burgers? Nobody! What summer barbeque would be complete without them?

Scale up the recipe if you want to feed a bunch of hungry kids or scale down if it is dinner for two.

Ingredients

- 1 tablespoon canola oil
- 1 medium sized onion
- 4 lettuce leaves
- 4 slices of tomato
- 2 tablespoons low fat mayonnaise
- 2 tablespoons tomato ketchup
- pound ground beef
- 1 teaspoon white vinegar
- 2 tablespoons steak sauce
- 4 sesame seed buns
- 2 teaspoons pickle relish
- 1/2 teaspoon ground pepper

Method

1. Heat the grill to medium high temperature. Put the onion, oil and 1 tablespoon ketchup in a saucepan and heat at a medium high temperature until the onion acquires a brown color. Lower the temperature to medium low and continue heating for another five minutes. Now combine mayonnaise, vinegar, relish and remaining ketchup in another bowl.

2. Meanwhile, add the beef, steak sauce and pepper to the already roasted onion and divide it to form four patties. Now toast the buns on the oiled grill and turn them once to avoid overheating. Assemble the burgers on the grill and serve them with lettuce leaves, slices of tomato and tomato ketchup.

Did you know?

How do you like your burgers? Cooked all the way through or slightly pink in the center? Vary the thickness of the burger to suit your tastes. If you prefer it well done, flatten the patty more. If you prefer it rarer, make the patty smaller in circumference and thicker.

3. Green Chili Bison Burger

If you love burgers with a touch of fire, this is for you. Bison meat is not as common as meat but tastes great when paired with chilis and grilled.

If you are not quite as adventurous, you can swap out the bison meat for regular ground beef but I do urge you to try this South American recipe as it was intended.

Ingredients

- Quarter cup sliced red onion
- One-pound ground bison
- 8 ounces of green chili
- Half a cup of shredded cheese
- Quarter teaspoon salt
- Quarter teaspoon ground pepper
- 4 hamburger buns
- 1 cup sliced lettuce

Method

1. Heat the grill to a medium high temperature range and put the onions in a bowl filled with water and cover it for some time. Place the bison, chili, shredded cheese, salt and ground pepper in a separate bowl and mix the contents.

2. Form the mixture into 4 patties. Oil the grill and place the bison, cheese, chili combination on it and cook it at a medium high temperature. Turn the patties one by one and give each side about five minutes on the grill.

3. Put the remaining chili and cheese on the burger and heat it till the cheese melts. Assemble the patties on the buns and serve the burgers with the lettuce leaves and onion.

Did you know?

Bison meat is more like game than regular beef and so has a leaner, more intense flavor. It makes a great addition to any game day celebration.

4. Grilled Fish Tacos

Choose fish fillets that are thinner to reduce the cooking time here and to make sure that everything cooks evenly. Instead of frying the fish, you are going to put it on the hot grill. This gives it a delicious light and smoky flavor that is impossible to get when you deep fry it.

Ingredients

- 2 tablespoons lime juice
- 2 tablespoons olive oil
- 4 teaspoons chili powder
- 1 teaspoon salt
- 1 teaspoon garlic powder
- 1 teaspoon onion powder
- Half teaspoon ground pepper
- 2 pounds Pacific halibut
- Quarter cup low fat sour cream
- Quarter cup low fat mayonnaise

Method

1. Heat the grill to a medium high temperature. Mix the fish with lime juice, olive oil, chili powder, garlic powder, onion powder, salt and pepper in a bowl and let it be for up to 30 minutes to allow the fish to catch the flavor.

2. To make coleslaw, mix the low-fat cream, low fat mayonnaise, salt, ground pepper, lime juice and sugar and refrigerate it until the tacos are completely cooked.

3. Now oil the grill and put the marinated fish on it and change the sides of the fish every five minutes to ensure balanced cooking. At the end, divide the fish into medium sized pieces and serve with coleslaw.

Did you know?

Taco is a traditional Mexican dish which has been eaten by the natives of Mexico since before the arrival of the Europeans in South America.

5. Grilled Chicken with a Touch of Chili and Lime

This recipe is cooked by using the butterflying technique which has become very popular over the last few decades. In this method, the chicken is grilled over direct heat at first and is then cooked over indirect heat. This aids in cooking the meat equally on the outside as well as the inside.

Ingredients

- 3 tablespoons chili powder
- 2 tablespoons lime zest
- 2 tablespoons olive oil
- 1 teaspoon oregano
- 1 tablespoon crushed garlic
- Three tablespoons lime juice
- One and a half teaspoon salt
- One teaspoon ground pepper
- 3½ to 4 pounds chicken

Method

1. Mix chili powder, lime zest, olive oil, oregano, garlic, lime juice, salt and pepper in a bowl to form a paste. Now cut the chicken in such a way that its backbone is completely removed and the remaining pieces can be spread out into a butterfly-like shape.

Marinate the chicken with the wet sauce prepared in the first step. Place a bowl or a dish over the chicken and refrigerate for at least 24 hours.

2. Heat half the grill to a medium high temperature and place the marinated chicken pieces on the grill. Turn the pieces every five minutes to ensure balanced cooking. When the pieces turn brown, remove them and put them in a platter. Serve the grilled chicken with tomato ketchup, onions and tomato slices.

Did you know?

Grilled chicken with chili and lime serves you with 25 percent of your daily vitamin A requirement. This vitamin is essential for the normal functioning of eyes, teeth, bone metabolism and immunity.

Read This FIRST - 100% FREE BONUS

FOR A LIMITED TIME ONLY – Get Olivia's best-selling book *"The #1 Cookbook: Over 170+ of the Most Popular Recipes Across 7 Different Cuisines!"* absolutely FREE!

Readers have absolutely loved this book because of the wide variety of recipes. It is highly recommended you check these recipes out and see what you can add to your home menu!

Once again, as a big thank-you for downloading this book, I'd like to offer it to you *100% FREE for a LIMITED TIME ONLY!*

Get your free copy at:

TheMenuAtHome.com/Bonus

6. Steak, Potato Kebabs and Cilantro Sauce

To add to the nutritional value of a well-cooked steak, it is served with potatoes, onions, salads and a delicious cilantro sauce in this recipe. The potatoes are precooked in a microwave oven and then grilled with the steak so that both the parts of the meal are ready at the exact same time.

Ingredients

- Half a cup of crushed cilantro leaves
- 2 tablespoons vinegar
- 2 tablespoons low fat sour cream
- 1 teaspoons chili powder
- Half teaspoon salt
- 8 small red potatoes
- A quarter pound strip steak
- 1 teaspoon olive oil
- 1 yellow bell pepper, quartered
- One large sweet onion

Method

1. Take the cilantro leaves, vinegar, sour cream, chili powder and salt in a bowl, mix it and set it aside. Heat the grill to a medium high temperature range. Put the potatoes in a microwave and allow them to get soft on heating for about three minutes.

2. Take the potatoes, steak, pepper, salt and oil in another bowl and mix the contents well. Put the steak, potatoes, peppers and onions on the skewers and grill them for about five minutes. Turn the skewers after every five minutes and make sure that the steak and potatoes are cooked evenly. Serve the dish with the sauce which was prepared in the first step.

Did you know?

This recipe is rich in zinc and fulfills more than 35 percent of the daily requirements. A deficiency of zinc in the human body can result in diseases related to liver, diabetes and other chronic illnesses.

7. Moroccan Shrimp with Spinach

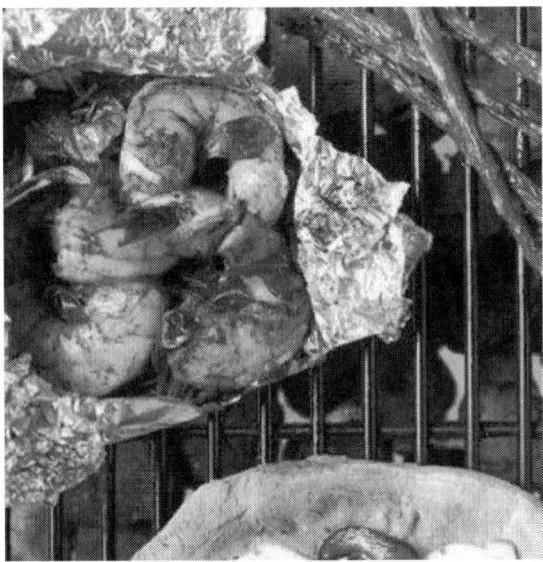

This African recipe has spinach as its primary ingredient and also includes shrimp grilled to perfection. The preparation time for this dish is a bit longer than the cooking time but you can do most of the work ahead of time. It takes less than 10 minutes to cook these.

Ingredients

- Half teaspoon coriander
- Half teaspoon cumin
- Half teaspoon paprika
- Quarter teaspoon salt
- 1 Pound large deveined and peeled shrimp
- 10 ounces spinach
- 3 tablespoons olive oil

Method

1. First of all, mix the coriander, cumin, paprika and salt in a small bowl until thoroughly combined. Put the shrimp in another bowl and coat it in the mixture of the spices, allow it to rest for at least thirty minutes in a covered container in the refrigerator.

2. Now, put the spinach, oil and salt in another large bowl, mix it and place it evenly on a sheet of aluminum along with the shrimp. Bring the edges of the foil together and seal them so that the whole package becomes airtight.

3. Now, put the aluminum sheets on the grill and start heating it. Allow the shrimp and spinach to be cooked for another five to seven minutes and wait until the shrimp becomes opaque. Serve the dish with sauces and tomato ketchup.

Did you know?

Aluminum foil grilling is a type of indirect grilling. This is done to prevent the meat and fire from coming into direct contact with each other. Indirect grilling is done in order to preserve the nutritional value of food and for stopping it from being overcooked.

8. Grilled Steak Served with Fresh Corn Salad

The key to having the perfect meal here is to prepare the ingredients of the salad beforehand. Then you can grill the steak and mix the salad to serve them both together while the steak is still fresh and juicy.

Ingredients

- 1 tablespoon garlic
- 3 teaspoons olive oil
- Half teaspoon salt
- 2 trimmed boneless strip pounds (1.25 pounds)
- 5 ears husked corn
- 2 chopped medium sized tomatoes
- 1 small red bell pepper
- 2 tablespoons basil
- 2 tablespoons vinegar

Method

1. Heat the grill to high temperature. Mix together garlic, some oil and a quarter teaspoon salt. Apply this blend on the sides of the steaks. Put the steak and corn on the grill for 2 to 4 minutes each side. Let the steak rest while the corn is cooked.

2. Keep cooking the corn; turn it to spread the heat all around the corn equally until some of the kernels are charred. This should take

around 8 minutes. Now take it off and give it about 5 minutes so that they become cool enough to handle.

3. Use a knife to remove the kernels of the corn cob. Mix the corn with tomatoes and pepper; and then stir in the basil, vinegar, salt and oil. Finish the steak by slicing them and serve them together with the salad.

Did You Know?

Although it has been 500,000 years since the first piece of meat was been grilled, grilling as a preferred cooking method did not become very common until the middle of the 20th century.

9. Smoky Ham and Corn Salad

Fresh corn, chopped deli ham and crispy croutons are mixed with a smoky, rich dressing in this light summer salad. Best served with a crisp glass of sliced melon and rosé.

Ingredients

- A one-third cup of sour cream
- 2 tablespoons of vinegar
- A teaspoon of paprika
- One-quarter teaspoon of salt
- A medium sized tomato
- A cup of corn kernels; fresh
- A cup of whole grain croutons
- Three-fourth of a cup diced ham

Method

1. Firstly, whisk sour cream in a bowl. Then add some vinegar, paprika and salt in the bowl. Try to use a large one to ensure that all the ingredients mix together really well.

2. Now add salad greens to the mixture. Finally finish by adding the diced tomato, corn kernels, croutons and ham. Mix all the ingredients really well.

Fun Fact

Ham is one of the oldest meats in human civilization. It is claimed that the French invented the treatment of pork to produce ham.

10. Grilled Steak with Pepper Relish

Bell peppers are mixed in vinaigrette and grilled in a foil package at the same time as the steak is grilled. It is served with corn.

Ingredients

- 3 small sliced bell peppers
- 1 halved and sliced small onion
- 2 tablespoons of vinegar; preferably balsamic
- 1 tablespoon of olive oil
- 1 tablespoon of rinsed capers
- 1 tablespoon fresh thyme; freshly chopped or 1 teaspoon dried and divided thyme
- Half teaspoon salt
- Half teaspoon of ground pepper
- A pound of sirloin steak; preferably 1-1.25 inches thick. Cut into four portions
- A teaspoon of garlic powder

Method

1. Heat the grill to a medium level. Mix the peppers with oil, vinegar, capers, 2 of the teaspoons of fresh thyme and a quarter teaspoon of each pepper and salt in a bowl.

2. Lay out the two and a half feet foil and put the mixture of pepper earlier made on one half. Now fold the foil and make sure that the foil is sealed properly so that the mixture does not leak during the grilling.

3. Now apply some garlic powder, quarter teaspoon of salt and pepper on each side of the steak. Oil the grill rack. You can do this by folding a paper towel, oiling it, holding it with tongs and rubbing it on the rack.

4. Now, place the packed foil and the steak on the grill. Grill the steak for 4 to 5 minutes per side. Grill the foil packet for 10 to 12 minutes during which time the vegetables should be tender. Now allow the steak to rest on the grill (no heat) for 5 minutes. Serve the juicy steak along with the peppers.

Did You Know?

Grilling meat is one of the best cooking methods because it intensifies the flavor of the meat.

11. Mojito-Rubbed Chicken with Grilled Pineapple

You can give the typical grilled chicken a twist with some added lime and mint!

Ingredients

- 4 chicken breast halves; skinless and boneless
- 2 limes
- 1 tablespoon of olive oil
- A medium sized pineapple
- 0.25 c. fresh mint leaves; loosely packed
- Pepper and salt

Method

1. Prepare the grill on medium. Use a meat mallet to beat the chicken to a flat half an inch thickness. Wrap the chicken between two plastic wrap sheets before pounding it.

2. Use 1 lime to squeeze two tablespoons of juice and a teaspoon of peel. Then cut the other lime into four pieces. Set these aside for now. Combine oil, juice, peel and lime together in a bowl.

3. Now brush the pineapple softly on each of the two sides with the lime mixture earlier prepared. Set aside the remaining mixture. Now place these slices of pineapple on the hot grill. Cook for 10

minutes. After the 10 minutes, both sides should turn brown. During the cooking, make sure that you turn it over once.

4. Now pull out the mixture of lime left earlier. Add some mint into it and apply it to the sides of the chicken. Season both sides of the chicken by sprinkling half a teaspoon of salt and a quarter teaspoon of ground pepper on both sides.

5. Now cook the chicken on a hot grill for about 5 minutes. The chicken should turn brown on both of the sides. It is served with wedges of lime and pineapple.

Did You Know?

Back in 1980, about 10 percent of a chicken's weight was from breast meat. In 2007, the percentage of breast meat in a chicken's total meat was 21 percent.

12. Spiced Pork Tenderloins with Mango Salsa

Add a delicious Mango Salsa to a dish as loved as Spiced Pork Tenderloins and you have the most exciting combination of dishes you can have.

Ingredients

- 2 mangoes; medium sized ripe
- 2 kiwifruits; medium sized
- 2 tablespoons vinegar
- 1 tablespoon fresh ginger; grated and peeled
- 1 tablespoon cilantro leaves
- 2 pork tenderloins
- 3 tablespoons of flour
- A teaspoon of salt
- A teaspoon of cumin; ground
- A teaspoon of coriander; ground
- Half teaspoon of cinnamon; ground
- Half teaspoon of ginger; ginger

Method

1. First, prepare the Mango Salsa. Mix mangoes, vinegar, cilantro, kiwifruit and ginger in a medium sized bowl. The aforementioned

ingredients make about 4 cups. If it is not being served right after being prepared, cover and refrigerate it for up to 4 hours. Preheat the grill for grilling over medium level heat.

2. Cut the pork tenderloins in half lengthwise. Make sure that you do not cut all the way through the meat. Take plastic wrap sheets and place each one between two sheets. Use a meat mallet to pound the meat into flat quarter inch thickness.

3. Mix some flour, coriander, ground ginger, cinnamon, salt, cumin on paper. Now add the pork to this mixture to spice it up. Turn it over to ensure that the spice mixture sticks to the meat evenly on all sides.

4. Now put the spice mixture added pork on the preheated grill rack. Cook it until the meat loses its pink color and turns a light shade of brown. Turn over the pork once to cook it evenly on both sides. Serve the cooked pork with Mango Salsa.

Did You Know?

Pork has more protein than chicken and is high in zinc, iron and B-vitamins.

13. Steak Sandwich with Grilled Onion

Treat yourself with a classy steak sandwich optimized by the presence of the crisp, grilled onion.

Ingredients

- A tablespoon of brown sugar
- A teaspoon of thyme leaves; fresh
- A beef steak
- A red onion, medium sized
- 8 slices of sourdough bread
- 2 ripe tomatoes; medium sized
- A bunch of arugula
- Quarter cup of soy sauce
- Quarter cup of vinegar; balsamic
- Quarter teaspoon of pepper; ground

Method

1. Use a plastic bag that is self-sealing to ensure that nothing leaks out. Pour mix soy sauce, pepper, thyme, vinegar and sugar into this plastic bag. Marinade steak by adding steak into this mixture. Turn it over to ensure even application. Now place the bag on a plate and let it rest for about fifteen minutes. Turn it over a few times.

2. Now preheat the grill to medium heat. To help in the handling, insert a metal skewer through the slices of the onion and set it aside.

3. Now remove the steak from the marinade and pour the marinade into a pan. Boil the marinade for two minutes by heating it over high heat.

4. Now put the slices of onion and the steak on the grill for around twelve to fifteen minutes. Cover the grill for better heating. When the onions turn brown and the meat loses its pink color, it is done. During the heating, keep applying the marinade and keep turning it over from time to time to make sure that it is heated evenly on both sides.

5. Once done, move the steak from the grill and take it to the cutting board. Now divide the cooked onion into rings.

6. Finally, slice the steak across its grain. Take four slices of bread and place the sliced steak and rings of onion on it. If there are any meat juices left over on the cutting board, pour them over the steak and the onion. Finish the dressing with tomatoes, arugula and the other four bread slices.

Did You Know?

As far as grilled foods are concerned, burgers (85 percent) and steak (80 percent) are the most popular dishes.

14. Juicy Rosemary Chicken Skewer Kabobs

This delicious Kabob recipe is really delicious and extremely tender, with the kabobs almost melting on your tongue. Even the pickiest eater won't be able to stay away from it!

Ingredients

- 1 cup extra virgin olive oil
- 1 cup ranch dressing
- 6 tablespoons Worcestershire sauce
- 2 tablespoons fresh rosemary, minced
- 4 teaspoons salt
- 2 teaspoons fresh lemon juice
- 2 teaspoons white vinegar
- 1/2 teaspoon ground black pepper, or to taste
- 2 tablespoons white sugar, or to taste
- 10 boneless and skinless chicken breast halves, cubed

Method

1. Place the ranch dressing, olive oil, rosemary, Worcestershire sauce, lemon juice, salt, pepper, white vinegar and sugar in a medium sized bowl and give it a stir.

2. Set the bowl aside for about 5 to 7 minutes, so that the sugar easily dissolves. Place the boneless chicken breast cubes in the bowl with the marinade and toss to quote. Cover using a cling wrap and place in the refrigerator for about 30 minutes.

3. Turn the grill on a medium-high heat and let it preheat while the chicken marinates. Thread the marinated chicken cubes onto greased skewers and discard the remaining marinade.

4. Spray the grill with some cooking spray. Place the prepared skewers on the greased grill and cook the skewers for about 10 to 12 minutes or until the center of the chicken is no longer pink. Serve hot with a side of your favorite condiment!

Did you know?

It is common knowledge that marinating meats before cooking ensures that the meat cooks easily. But, if you are cooking smaller pieces of meat, do not marinate the meat for too long, or else the meat will get over tender and fall apart on the grill.

15. Grilled Garlic and Pepper Steak with a Caprese Salad

This delicious garlic and pepper flavored steak tastes delicious with a side of the delicious and healthy salad makes for a healthy and nutritious meal. This recipe is for 8 portions.

Ingredients

- 4 tomatoes, cut into cubes
- 8 ounces fresh mozzarella, chopped into 1-inch cubes
- 1/2 cup fresh basil, roughly chopped
- 2 cloves of garlic, minced (you may add more for added flavor)
- 2 tablespoons extra virgin olive oil
- 2 pounds lean flank steak
- 2 cloves of garlic, minced
- 2 tablespoons extra virgin olive oil
- Salt, to taste
- freshly ground black pepper, to taste
- 1 ½ cup lettuce
- 1/4 cup balsamic vinegar, or to taste
- Extra virgin olive oil, to taste

Method

1. In a large mixing bowl, combine together the basil, mozzarella cheese, 2 minced garlic cloves and the 2 tablespoons of extra virgin olive oil and toss well to coat. Cover the bowl using a cling

wrap and place in the refrigerator. Turn the grill up to medium-high heat and preheat it for a few minutes. Spray the grill with some cooking oil.

2. Take a large re-sealable bag and place the 2 minced garlic cloves, 2 tablespoons extra virgin olive oil, pepper and salt in it. Place the steak in the bag and seal the bag. Shake the bag well to evenly distribute the marinade mixture on the steak.

3. Place the steak on the greased grill and cook them to your taste. For a medium steak cook the steak for about 5 minutes on each side. A kitchen thermometer inserted in the center of the steak should read 140 degrees Fahrenheit (about 60 degrees Celsius). Once the steak is taken off the grill, let the steak sit out for about 5 minutes and then slice it against the grain.

4. Remove the salad from the refrigerator and divide the lettuce among 8 serving plates. Spoon the balsamic vinegar and olive oil onto the serving plates. Place about 1/8 of the grilled steak on the lettuce and top with about 1/8 of the prepared salad on the steak.

Did you know?

If you have unexpected guests or a recipe that won't stretch quite far enough, serving a simple green salad as a starter will blunt your guest's appetites and help them to feel fuller more quickly.

16. Quick and Easy Italian Grilled Chicken

This is the quickest and easiest way to marinade and cook chicken, ideal for new cooks.

Ingredients

- 8 boneless and skinless chicken breast halves
- 2 teaspoons garlic powder
- 4 cups Italian-style salad dressing of your choice
- 2 teaspoons salt

Method

1. Combine the garlic powder and salad dressing in a medium sized bowl. Add in the salt and mix well. Place the chicken breast halves in this mix and keep turning them to coat well. Cover the bowl using a cling wrap and place in the refrigerator for about 4 hours. It is preferable to marinate overnight for best results!

2. Turn the grill up to the highest heat and let the grill preheat. Spray the grill with some cooking spray. Drain the excess marinade from the chicken and place the breast halves on the greased grill.

3. Grill the chicken breasts for about 8 minutes on each side. Remove from grill and let it rest for a few minutes, before slicing it against the grain. Serve hot with a side of your favorite condiment.

Did you know?

The garlic powder used in this recipe has all the properties of fresh garlic and helps with the reduction of the cholesterol levels in the body.

17. Paprika Shrimp with Lemon Aioli

Though the list of ingredients in this recipe may make the dish seem to be extremely bland and tasteless, the cured lemons have an extremely intense flavor that adds to the dish. If you would like some extra flavor for the dish, add some hot pepper or garlic in it.

Ingredients

- 4 slices of cured lemon
- 1 cup mayonnaise
- 2 tablespoons fresh tarragon, minced
- 2 teaspoons lemon juice
- 2 pounds extra-large shrimp, peeled and deveined
- 4 teaspoons extra virgin olive oil
- 2 teaspoons smoked paprika
- 1 teaspoon kosher salt

Method

1. Pour some cold water in a small bowl and soak the cured lemons in it for about 10 minutes, in order to get rid of the curing brine. Place the drained lemons on an absorbent towel to dry. Mince the lemon finely. In a small mixing bowl combine the mayonnaise, lemon juice, tarragon and minced lemon together. Cover the bowl using a cling wrap and refrigerate until chilled. If you do not have too long, refrigerate for at least 15 minutes.

2. Turn up your grill to high heat and let it preheat for at least 10 minutes. Spray some cooking spray on the grill to grease it. Place the peeled and deveined shrimp in a bowl and pour the extra virgin

olive oil over them. Lightly sprinkle the kosher salt and smoked paprika on the shrimp and mix well until the shrimp are well coated.

3. Place the marinated shrimp on the greased and preheated grill and cook for about 2 minutes on each side or until they get a bright pink tinge and the meat loses its transparency. Serve hot with the prepared lemon aioli.

Did you know?

Lemons aid in restoring the natural pH levels in the body and aid in the detoxification of the digestive system. Lemons also aid in smooth digestion and prevent the occurrence of constipation in the body.

18. Chicken Souvlaki with a Delicious Tzatziki Sauce

Souvlaki is a traditional Greek dish which contains grilled vegetables and meats and is usually served with a dipping sauce. These delicious kabobs have a delicious Greek flavor and the marinade can also be used to flavor other meats like beef and pork too!

Ingredients

- 1/2 cup extra virgin olive oil
- 1/4 cup lemon juice
- 4 cloves of garlic, crushed
- 2 teaspoons dried oregano
- 1 teaspoon salt
- 3 pounds chicken breast halves, boneless and skinless, chopped into small pieces

For the Sauce

- 1 ½ cups Greek-style yogurt, unflavored
- 1 cucumber, peeled, seeds removed and grated
- 2 tablespoons extra virgin olive oil
- 4 teaspoons white vinegar
- 2 cloves of garlic, minced
- 2 pinches of salt
- 12 wooden skewers, or as you need

Method

1. Pour the ½ cup extra virgin olive oil into a re-sealable bag. Add in the 4 minced garlic cloves, 1 teaspoon salt and the 2 teaspoons of

dried oregano. Place the chicken in the bag, seal it and slowly shake it up to ensure that the chicken is well coated with the marinade. Place the bag in the refrigerator and let the chicken marinate for about 3 to 4 hours.

2. While the chicken marinates, prepare the dipping sauce. Pour the yogurt in to a small mixing bowl. Add in the grated cucumber, the 2 tablespoons extra virgin olive oil, white vinegar, the 2 cloves of minced garlic and the salt to it. Mix well and place the prepared tzatziki sauce in the refrigerator. Chill for at least 3 hours.

3. Turn up your grill on a medium high flame and let it preheat for a few minutes. Grease the grill with some cooking spray. Place the skewers in some warm water and let them soak for 15 to 20 minutes.

4. Remove the marinated pieces of chicken and thread them onto the prepared skewers. Drain and discard the leftover marinade.

5. Place the prepared skewers on the greased and preheated grill. Keep turning the skewers frequently so that the chicken is evenly browned from all sides. It should take about 10 minutes. Serve hot with the prepared tzatziki sauce.

Did you know?

The tzatziki is a delicious Greek dipping sauce and it goes amazingly well with all kinds of meat preparations. The traditional dipping sauce usually uses yoghurt made using the milk from goats and sheep.

19. Sweet and Spicy Grilled Pork Tenderloin

This delicious rub gives the pork tenderloins a sweet and spicy flavor. Just marinate the tenderloins and leave them for a few minutes. Grill and you are good to go!

Ingredients

- 2 teaspoons onion powder
- 2 teaspoons garlic powder
- 6 tablespoons chipotle chili powder
- 1 tablespoon salt
- 1/2 cup brown sugar
- 4 pork tenderloins, each about ¾ pound

Method

1. Turn up your grill to a medium high flame and coat it with some cooking spray. Take a large re-sealable bag and add the garlic powder, onion powder, salt, brown sugar and chipotle chili powder to it. Place the tenderloins in the bag with the marinade and shake the bag to evenly coat the tenderloin with the marinade. Place the bag in the refrigerator for about 20 minutes.

2. Place the pork tenderloins on the greased grill and cook for about 20 to 25 minutes. Make sure to turn over the tenderloins every 7 minutes. Once done, remove the tenderloins from the grill and let them rest for about 10 minutes before slicing it. Serve hot.

Did you know?

Pork tenderloin is a wonderfully juicy cut of meat without a huge amount of fat on it. It is perfect for grilling.

20. Bacon Stuffed Zucchini Boats

Stuffed grilled zucchini that makes a delicious appetizer or a light meal!

Ingredients

- 4 medium zucchinis
- 2 slices white bread, cut into bite sizes
- 1/2 cup bacon, crumbled
- 2 tablespoons black olives, minced finely
- 2 jalapeno peppers, minced
- 6 tablespoons green chili peppers, diced
- 1/2 cup onion, minced
- 1/2 cup tomato, chopped
- 3/4 cup Cheddar cheese, shredded
- 2 pinches dried basil
- salt to taste
- ground black pepper to taste

Method

1. Prepare the grill in order to indirectly heat the zucchini boats. Pour enough water to cover the zucchini in a pot. Heat the pot until the water is boiling and let the zucchini cook for another 5 minutes. Drain the zucchini and cool completely before cutting them

lengthwise in halves. Using a small spoon, spoon out the flesh of the zucchini and chop the pulp.

2. Combine the prepared zucchini pulp, crumbled bacon, bread pieces, jalapenos, olives, onions, green chili peppers, Cheddar cheese and tomato in a bowl. Add in the basil, salt and pepper.

3. Spoon the prepared filling mix into the scooped-out zucchini halves. Cover the zucchini halves with some foil to seal them. Place the prepared zucchini boats on the prepared grill and cook them for about 20 minutes or until the zucchini is tender to touch. Serve hot.

Did you know?

Zucchini has no saturated fats in it. It is an extremely good source of dietary fibers and helps prevent the cancer of the colon.

21. Rosemary Stuffed, Bacon Wrapped Chicken

This recipe is ideal for the days when you are in no mood to do a lot of prep. Grill it up and serve with a side of some rice and grilled veggies.

Ingredients

- 8 teaspoons garlic powder
- 8 chicken breast halves, skinless and boneless
- Salt, to taste
- Pepper, to taste
- 8 sprigs fresh rosemary
- 8 thick slices bacon

Method

1. Turn up your grill on a medium high flame and lightly spray the grill with some cooking spray. Dust a teaspoon of garlic powder on a single chicken breast. Sprinkle salt and pepper and place a rosemary sprig on it. Take the slice of bacon and wrap it around the chicken breast in order to secure the rosemary sprig in place. Secure the bacon in place using a toothpick.

2. Place the prepared chicken breast on the prepared grill and cook until the chicken is no longer pink in the center. This will take about 8 minutes per side. Remove the toothpicks and serve hot!

Did you know?

Rosemary is an extremely good source of anti-inflammatory compounds and anti-oxidants that help with the immune system of the body and also aids in healthy digestion.

22. Sweet n Spicy Grilled Pineapple Rings

If you are a sucker for sweet and spicy flavors, this will be your favorite dish in no time. Hot sauce cuts into the sweetness of the pineapple, giving it a delicious flavor that will leave you begging for more!

Ingredients

- 2 fresh pineapples, peeled, cored and cut into rings
- 1/2 teaspoon honey
- 6 tablespoons melted butter
- ¼ teaspoon hot pepper sauce
- salt to taste

Method

1. In a large re-sealable bag place the pineapple rings. Pour in the honey, hot pepper sauce, butter and salt and seal the bag. Shake the bag until the pineapple is well coated with the marinade. Leave it to marinate overnight.

2. Turn up your grill to the highest heat and lightly spray the grill with some cooking spray. Place the prepared pineapple pieces on the grill and cook for 3 minutes per side or until lightly tender. Serve immediately.

Did you know?

The acidic and stinging taste you get when you consume a pineapple is due to the presence of the Bromelain enzyme in it. The Bromelain enzyme breaks down protein; so, when you eat the pineapple, it eats you!

23. Hamburgers Topped with Mushrooms and Swiss Cheese

If you are tired of eating the regular ordinary hamburger, this recipe is your ticket to something mind-blowingly fantastic!

Ingredients

- 3/4-pound lean ground beef
- 1/4 teaspoon seasoned meat tenderizer
- Salt, to taste
- Pepper, to taste
- 1 teaspoon butter
- 1 (4 ounce) can sliced mushrooms, drained
- 1 tablespoon soy sauce
- 3 slices Swiss cheese
- 3 hamburger buns

Method

1. Turn on the grill to medium high heat and spray it with some cooking spray. Divide the lean ground beef into 3 parts and shape into patties. Sprinkle the salt, pepper and meat tenderizer on them and keep aside.

2. Place the butter in a skillet and heat over a medium flame until it has melted. Add in the drained mushrooms and the soy sauce and

toss well until the mushrooms are browned. Take off heat but keep warm.

3. Place the prepared patties on the grill and cook for about 8 minutes on each side. Distribute the prepared mushrooms on the patties and place one slice of cheese on each patty. Cover the grill and cook for one minute or until the cheese melts. Remove from grill, place on the hamburger buns and serve hot!

Did you know?

The 28th of May every year is celebrated as National Hamburger Day!

24. Tandoori Chicken Thighs

With the freshness of yogurt, this spicy dish will sure leave you yearning for more!

Ingredients

- ¾ cup plain yogurt
- 1 teaspoon kosher salt
- 1/2 teaspoon black pepper corns
- 1/4 teaspoon cloves, ground
- 1 tablespoon ginger, freshly grated
- 1-1/2 cloves garlic, minced
- 2 teaspoons paprika
- 1 teaspoon cumin, ground
- 1 teaspoon cinnamon, ground
- 1 teaspoon coriander seeds, ground
- 8 chicken thighs
- Olive oil spray

Method

1. Combine the yogurt, pepper corns, kosher salt, ground cloves and grated ginger and mix well. Add in the cinnamon, paprika, coriander seeds, garlic and cumin to it. Keep aside.

2. Rinse the chicken and pat dry. Take a large re-sealable bag and place the chicken in it. Add the prepared yoghurt mix to it and seal the bag. Shake a few times to distribute the marinade and refrigerate overnight.

3. Turn up the grill to medium and let it preheat. Drain the marinade from the chicken and discard the extra marinade. Spray some olive oil on the chicken pieces and place on the preheated grill.

4. Cook the chicken for 2 minutes on each side. Arrange the grill so that the chicken can get indirect heat. Keep cooking the chicken for another 40 minutes. Serve hot with some yogurt and cucumber dip.

Did you know?

The tandoor is traditionally an oven made of clay, used to grill meats and bake breads. The dishes made in a traditional tandoor have a distinct flavor that they get from being cooked in the clay oven.

25. Honey Flavored Grilled Shrimp

This recipe is ideal for the days when you want to make a quick and delicious dish without putting in hours of work!

Ingredients

- 2 pounds medium sized shrimp, peeled and deveined
- 1 cup chili-garlic sauce
- 1 cup honey
- 12 bamboo skewers, soaked in water for 20 minutes

Method

1. Turn the grill up on a medium high heat and lightly spray cooking spray on the grill. Combine the honey and chili-garlic sauce in a small bowl. Skewer the shrimp on the soaked bamboo skewers, with the skewer going through the head and coming out through the tail side.

2. Place the skewers on the greased grill and grill the shrimp, while constantly basting it with the prepared sauce mix. Keep grilling until the shrimps until they are firm and get a pink tinge to them. This will take about 10 minutes. Serve hot!

Did you know?

Honey is one of the only foods in the world that doesn't spoil; in fact, archaeologists have found jars of honey in ancient Egyptian tombs and this honey is still edible!

26. Spicy Asian Pork Skewers

These kabobs are quick to prepare, with the Teriyaki sauce giving them an intense Asian flavor.

Ingredients

- 4 tablespoons teriyaki sauce
- 2 tablespoons red wine vinegar
- 2 tablespoons vegetable oil
- 2 teaspoons brown sugar
- 1 teaspoon red pepper flakes
- 1-1/2 pounds pork tenderloin, cut into 1-inch cubes

Method

1. Combine the teriyaki sauce, vegetable oil, pepper flakes, red wine vinegar and brown sugar in a medium sized bowl. Add the cubed pork tenderloin and toss well, until coated. Marinate overnight or a minimum of 30 – 45 minutes.

2. Turn up your grill to high and preheat. Lightly spray cooking oil on the grill. Thread the marinated pork cubes on to skewers and place on the grill. Cook for about 12 minutes, constantly rotating the skewers and basting them with the leftover marinade. Serve hot!

Did you know?

Teriyaki is actually a technique used in Japanese cooking. It consists of grilling or broiling meats that are coated with a mixture of mirin, soy sauce and sugar.

27. Sweet and Savory Salmon on the Grill

The intense flavor of this dish consists of a perfect balance between the marinade and the fish, neither overpowering the other.

Ingredients

- 3 pounds salmon fillets
- garlic powder, to taste
- lemon pepper, as per taste
- salt, as per taste
- 2/3 cup brown sugar
- 2/3 cup soy sauce
- 2/3 cup water
- 1/2 cup oil

Method

1. Sprinkle the garlic powder, lemon pepper and salt on the salmon fillets. Combine the brown sugar, vegetable oil, soy sauce and water in a small bowl. Keep stirring until the sugar melts.

2. Place the seasoned salmon filets in a large re-sealable bag and pour the prepared marinade mix onto it. Shake the bag to coat and refrigerate for 2 hours.

3. Turn the grill up to medium heat and let it preheat. Spray the cooking spray on the grill. Place the marinated salmon on the grill and cook for 8 minutes per side or until the fish flakes away when cut with a fork. Serve hot!

Did you know?

Salmon is considered to be one of the healthiest fishes in the world as it is extremely rich in vitamin B12, amino acids, proteins and omega-3 fatty acids. Serve it with a side of a salad and you've got a highly nutritional meal on your hands.

28. Delicious Black Bean Patties

Take a break from the frozen veggie burgers and try this recipe; you will never go back to the frozen aisle for these again!

Ingredients

- 1 onion, finely chopped
- 2 (16 ounce) cans black beans, drained and rinsed
- 2 tablespoons chili powder
- 2 teaspoons Thai chili sauce or hot sauce
- 1 green bell pepper, finely chopped
- 6 cloves garlic, finely chopped
- 1 cup bread crumbs
- 2 eggs
- 2 tablespoons cumin

Method

1. Turn up your grill to high heat and spray some cooking spray on the grill. Place a piece of aluminum foil on it. Add the black beans to a medium sized bowl and mash them using a fork until they are thick and mushy. Add the onion, bell pepper and garlic to it and mix well.

2. Combine the egg, cumin, chili powder and chili sauce together in a small bowl. Pour this mix into the black bean mix and mix well. Add in the bread crumbs and mix until the mixture can hold together.

3. Divide the mix into 8 patties. Place the patties on the foil and grill for about 8 minutes on each side. Place in burger buns and serve immediately or refrigerate for later use.

Did you know?

Black beans aid the digestive system and reduce the risk of colon cancer! Just be sure to soak the dry beans overnight to reduce the chance of them causing too much wind in the digestive tract.

29. Honey Chicken and Vegetable Skewers

This sweet and tangy recipe is loved by all! You can substitute the usual components of an outdoor barbeque with this delicious and fresh recipe.

Ingredients

- 2 tablespoons vegetable oil
- 8 teaspoons honey
- 8 teaspoons soy sauce
- 1/8 teaspoon ground black pepper
- 4 chicken breast halves, skinless and boneless - cut into 1-inch cubes
- 1 clove garlic
- 1 medium onion, cut into cubes
- 2 small red bell peppers, cut into cubes
- Skewers

Method

1. Combine the honey, black pepper, soy sauce and vegetable oil together in a large bowl. Spoon out a few teaspoons of the marinade into a smaller bowl and add the chicken pieces to the big bowl. Add in the red bell peppers, garlic and onion to the chicken and mix well. Refrigerate the bowl overnight or for at least 2 hours.

2. Turn the grill up on high heat and preheat. Drain the excess marinade and discard it. Skewer the chicken pieces and vegetables on the skewers, alternately.

3. Spray the grill with some cooking spray and place the skewers on the grill. Cook the skewers for about 150 minutes, constantly turning and brushing with the marinade set aside. Serve hot!

Did you know?

According to researchers, the cooking of meats over an open flame has had a catalytic effect on the evolution of the human brain! Keep barbequing!

30. Chicken Tikka Masala

Chicken Tikka Masala is a chicken steeped in a blend of spices and yogurt and served in a tomato based cream sauce. This dish is best served with a side of pita bread or on a bed of steamed rice.

Ingredients

- 2 cups yogurt
- 2 tablespoons lemon juice
- 4 teaspoons ground cumin
- 2 teaspoons ground cinnamon
- 4 teaspoons cayenne pepper
- 4 teaspoons black pepper, freshly ground
- 2 tablespoons fresh ginger, minced
- 8 teaspoons salt, or to taste
- 6 chicken breasts, skinless and boneless, cut into bite-size pieces
- 8 long skewers
- 2 tablespoons butter
- 2 cloves garlic, minced
- 2 jalapeno peppers, finely chopped
- 4 teaspoons ground cumin
- 4 teaspoons paprika
- 2 tablespoons salt, or to taste
- 2 cups canned tomato sauce
- 2 cups heavy cream
- 1/2 cup chopped fresh cilantro

Method

1. Mix together the lemon juice, yogurt, cinnamon, cumin, black pepper, cayenne pepper, salt and ginger in a large bowl. Add in the chicken and cover with cling wrap. Refrigerate for an hour.

2. Turn up your grill on high and preheat. Spray the grill with some cooking spray. Skewer the chicken pieces on the skewers and discard the excess marinade. Place on the grill and cook for 7 minutes on each side.

3. In a large skillet, melt the butter over a medium flame. Add the garlic and jalapeno and sauté for 1 minute. Add in the paprika, cumin and salt. Pour in the tomato sauce and heavy cream and mix well.

4. Once the gravy starts simmering, lower the heat and cook until the sauce thickens. Add in the grilled pieces of chicken and cook for another 10 minutes. Serve hot topped with some cilantro!

Did you know?

The grilled pieces of chicken are known as "tikkas" and are traditionally baked in a clay oven known as a tandoor.

31. Tangy Grilled Chicken

This easy to make dish is sweet and tangy and will end up as your and your family's favorite dish!

Ingredients

- 8 chicken breast halves, skinless and boneless
- 2 teaspoons steak sauce
- 2/3 cup Dijon mustard
- 1/4 cup mayonnaise
- 1/2 cup honey

Method

1. Turn up the grill on medium heat and let it preheat. Spray with some cooking oil. Combine the steak sauce, mustard, mayonnaise and honey in a bowl. Spoon out some for basting and add the chicken to the remaining marinade. Coat well and allow marinating for 30 minutes.

2. Set up the grill to indirectly heat and cook the chicken for about 20 minutes, turning the chicken on occasion. With each turn baste the chicken with the reserved marinade. Serve immediately!

Did you know?

Mayonnaise is a base for a variety of other sauces. For example, tartar sauce is a combination of pickled onions, mayonnaise and cucumber. Ranch dressing is prepared by combining buttermilk, finely minced onion and mayonnaise together.

32. Stuffed Jalapenos Wrapped in Bacon

Cream cheese stuffed jalapenos, covered with bacon and grilled to perfection!

Ingredients

- 12 fresh jalapeno peppers, cut into halves and seeds removed
- 2 (8 ounce) packages cream cheese
- 24 slices bacon

Method

1. Turn the grill up to high heat and spray it with cooking spray. Spoon the cream cheese into the jalapeno halves and wrap the bacon around the jalapeno halves.

2. Keep in place using a toothpick. Place the prepared jalapenos on the grill and grill until the bacon is crispy. Serve hot!

Did you know?

Jalapenos were the first peppers sent to space!

33. Grilled Garlic and Pepper Shrimp

This delicious dish is best served on a bed of freshly prepared pasta!

Ingredients

- 2 lemons, juiced
- 2 cups extra virgin olive oil
- 2 tablespoons tomato paste
- 2 teaspoons ground black pepper
- 4 tablespoons hot pepper sauce
- 1/2 cup fresh parsley, chopped
- 2 teaspoons salt
- 6 cloves garlic, minced
- 4 teaspoons dried oregano
- 4 pounds large shrimp, peeled and deveined with tails attached
- Skewers

Method

1. Combine the lemon juice, olive oil, tomato paste, black pepper, hot pepper sauce, parsley, salt, garlic and oregano together in a bowl. Spoon out some of the marinade and reserve for basting. Pour the marinade into a large re-sealable bag and add in the shrimp. Seal and shake to coat. Refrigerate for 2 hours.

2. Turn up your grill to medium high and coat the grill with some cooking spray. Drain the shrimp and thread them onto the skewers. Place the shrimp on the grill and cook for 7 minutes per side.

Frequently baste using the reserved marinade. Cook until opaque and serve hot.

Did you know?

To easily peel garlic just pop them into the microwave for 5 – 10 seconds. The skin will pop off and the flesh will become softer, making it easier to crush or mince it!

34. Honey Garlic Steaks

This delicious recipe gives you a delicious piece of savory steak that is so succulent it almost melts in the mouth!

Ingredients

- 1 cup balsamic vinegar
- 1/2 cup soy sauce
- 6 tablespoons minced garlic
- 4 tablespoons honey
- 4 tablespoons olive oil
- 4 teaspoons ground black pepper
- 2 teaspoons Worcestershire sauce
- 2 teaspoons onion powder
- 1 teaspoon salt
- 1 teaspoon liquid smoke flavoring
- 2 pinches cayenne pepper
- 4 (1/2 pound) rib-eye steaks

Method

1. Combine the soy sauce, vinegar, garlic, olive oil, honey, Worcestershire sauce, black pepper, salt, onion powder, cayenne pepper and liquid smoke in a bowl.

2. Place the steaks in the marinade and slowly rub the marinade into the steaks. Cover and refrigerate for 2 days. Turn up the grill to medium high and preheat. Spray cooking spray on the grill.

3. Place the steaks on the preheated grill and cook for about 7 minutes per side for a medium piece of steak. Serve hot with a side of grilled vegetables and mashed potatoes!

Did you know?

It is better to over season a steak while grilling as there is high probability that all the heavy seasoning will fall off the steak into the fire while you grill, resulting in an under seasoned steak.

35. Butter Basil Shrimp

The buttery goodness, when combined with the strong flavors of mustard and basil create a tantalizing magic of flavors on your tongue!

Ingredients

- 4 teaspoons extra virgin olive oil
- 8 teaspoons butter, melted
- 1 lemon, juiced
- 5 teaspoons Dijon mustard
- 1/4 cup fresh basil leaves, minced
- 2 cloves garlic, minced
- salt to taste
- white pepper, to taste
- 2 pounds fresh shrimp, peeled and deveined
- Skewers

Method

1. Combine the melted butter, olive oil, mustard, lemon juice, garlic and basil in a shallow dish. Season to taste with white pepper and salt. Add in the shrimps and toss well until well coated. Cover the dish and refrigerate for an hour or two.

2. Turn up the grill to high and spray the grill with some cooking spray. Drain the shrimp and thread them onto the skewers. Discard the extra marinate. Place the skewers on the grill and cook for about 5 minutes, frequently turning. Serve hot!

Did you know?

Basil is not only one of the healthiest herbs, with a rich content of vitamin A, but also is considered to be a holy plant in India, with women praying to it and watering it first thing every morning!

36. London Broil

The steak is so juicy, succulent and flavorful on its own; you won't feel the need to accompany it with condiments of any kind!

Ingredients

- 1/2 clove garlic, minced
- 1/2 teaspoon salt
- 4 1/2 teaspoons soy sauce
- 1 1/2 teaspoons ketchup
- 1 1/2 teaspoons vegetable oil
- 1/4 teaspoon ground black pepper
- 1/4 teaspoon dried oregano
- 2 pounds flank steak

Method

1. Combine the salt, garlic, ketchup, soy sauce, black pepper, vegetable oil and oregano in a small bowl. Rub the prepared marinate on the steak flanks and wrap in an aluminum foil. Refrigerate overnight, turning the steak over every few hours.

2. Turn up the grill to high and lightly grease the grill. Place the marinated steak on the grill and cook for about 7 minutes for a medium steak. Rest the steak for 5 minutes before slicing. Serve hot!

Did you know?

The London Broil originated in North America and is fairly unknown in the city it is named after!

37. Grilled Fish Tacos with A Zesty Lemon Dressing

These grilled fish tacos make for an ideal meal and taste delicious when served accompanied with a chipotle lime dressing that not only enhances the flavor of the tacos, but also add some zing to them! You can add or remove the toppings as per your taste

Ingredients

- 1/2 cup extra virgin olive oil
- 2 teaspoons seafood seasoning
- 1 tablespoon honey
- 1/4 cup distilled white vinegar
- 4 teaspoons lime zest
- 1/4 cup fresh lime juice
- 2 teaspoons hot pepper sauce, or to taste
- 4 cloves garlic, minced
- 1 teaspoon chili powder
- 1 teaspoon cumin
- 1 teaspoon ground black pepper
- 2 pounds tilapia fillets, cut into chunks

Dressing

- 2 cups light sour cream
- 1 cup adobo sauce
- 1/4 cup fresh lime juice
- 4 teaspoons lime zest
- 1/2 teaspoon cumin
- 1/2 teaspoon chili powder
- 1 teaspoon seafood seasoning
- Salt, to taste
- Pepper, to taste

Toppings

- 2 (10 ounce) packages tortillas
- 3 large ripe tomatoes, diced
- 2 bunches cilantro, chopped finely
- 1 large cabbage, cored and shredded
- 4 limes, cut in wedges

Method

1. Combine the extra virgin olive oil, lime juice, vinegar, honey, lime zest, cumin, garlic, seafood seasoning, chili powder, hot sauce and black pepper in a bowl. Whisk until the marinade is well blended.

2. Place the fish filets in a flat dish with raised sides and pour the prepared marinade over fillets. Cover the dish with some plastic wrap and place in a refrigerator for 8 to 10 hours.

3. To prepare the dressing, whisk together the adobo sauce and sour cream in a bowl until well blended. Add in the lime zest, lime juice, chili powder, cumin and seafood seasoning and mix well. Taste and add salt and pepper as per needed. Cover the bowl and place in the refrigerator to chill.

4. Turn up your grill on high heat and leave to preheat. Lightly spray the grill with some cooking spray and place it about 4 inches above the flame. Drain the fish from the marinade and discard the extra marinade. Place the marinated fish on the grill and cook for about 9 minutes, flipping over around the 4 and half minute mark or cook until the fish fillet easily flakes with a fork.

5. To assemble the tacos, place the grilled fish in the center of the tortillas. Top the fish with some chopped cilantro, cabbage and cilantro. Spoon some of the prepared dressing over the toppings and roll the tortillas around the fish and toppings. Serve immediately with some lemon wedges on the side.

Did you know?

The word taco means "light lunch" in Mexican Spanish and 3rd October is celebrated as National Taco Day.

38. Butter Beer Chicken

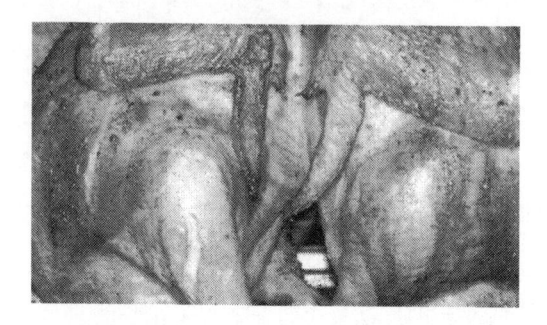

Cooking a whole chicken can often seem like a Herculean task, but the recipe makes the whole process as easy as snapping your fingers. The dish is a little unorthodox, but the final result is a delicious, moist and juicy meal! And despite the name, this chicken has nothing to do with the Harry Potter universe!

Ingredients

- 1/2 cup butter
- 6 ounces beer (discard the extra beer from the can)
- 1 tablespoon garlic salt
- 2-pound whole chicken
- 1 tablespoon paprika
- Salt, to taste
- Pepper, to taste

Method

1. Turn up your grill on a low heat and let the grill preheat. Heat a small skillet over a medium flame. Add in ¼ cup butter and melt it. Sprinkle in half the quantities of the garlic salt, salt, paprika and pepper in the melted butter and mix well.

2. Leave the beer in the can and pour in the remaining butter into the can with the beer. Add the remaining spices into the can. Once all the ingredients are in it, place the beer can on a use and throw baking sheet. Carefully place the chicken on the can by placing the can into the opening of the chicken. Using a pastry brush gently baste the chicken using the prepared seasoned melted butter mix.

3. Gently lift the baking sheet, ensuring that you do not disturb the placement of the can and the chicken, and place the baking sheet on the preheated grill. Cook the chicken on the low flame for about 3 to 3 and half hours or until a thermometer inserted in the center of the chicken reads 180 degrees Fahrenheit or about 80 degrees Celsius.

4. Just before serving, gently remove the can from the cavity. Take care; the can will be very hot, so use some sturdy tongs. Serve hot!

Did you know?

Beer contains a high level of silicone that helps in the strengthening of bones and contains almost all the nutrients that we need to survive.

39. Fiery Shrimp

If you need a quick meal fix, these shrimps will make your ideal go to meal!

Ingredients

- 2 large cloves garlic
- 1 teaspoon cayenne pepper
- 4 pounds large shrimp, peeled and deveined
- 2 tablespoons coarse salt
- 1/4 cup olive oil
- 2 teaspoons paprika
- 4 teaspoons lemon juice
- 16 wedges lemon, for garnish

Method

1. Turn up your grill to medium heat to preheat. Place the garlic with the salt in a bowl and crush. Add in the cayenne, paprika, lemon juice and olive oil to make a paste. Place the shrimp in a large bowl, add in the spicy paste and toss to coat.

2. Grease the grate with some oil and place the shrimp on it. Cook for about 3 minutes per side or until the shrimp turn opaque. Serve hot, garnished with some lemon wedges.

Did you know?

Cayenne pepper aids in weight loss by reducing appetite, increasing energy usage in the body and also helps in breaking down the fats in the body!

40. Bacon Wrapped Hamburgers

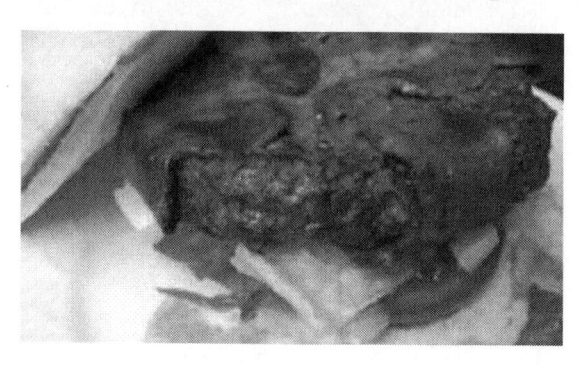

The name might sound weird, but the bacon in the patty makes the patty moist and tender!

Ingredients

- 1 cup Cheddar cheese, shredded
- 2 tablespoons Parmesan cheese, grated
- 2 small onions, finely chopped
- 2 eggs
- 2 tablespoons ketchup
- 2 tablespoons Worcestershire sauce
- 1 teaspoon salt
- 1/4 teaspoon pepper
- 2 pounds ground beef
- 12 slices bacon
- 12 hamburger buns, split

Method

1. Turn up your grill on high heat and let it preheat. Combine the Cheddar, Parmesan, eggs, onions, Worcestershire sauce, ketchup, pepper and salt in a large bowl, whisking well. Add in the ground beef, crumbling it into bits with your hands and mix well.

2. Divide into 12 equal parts and shape into patties. Take a slice of bacon and wrap it around the patty carefully, ensuring that you don't mess the shape of the patty. Fasten the bacon in place using a toothpick.

3. Grease the grill with some cooking spray and place the patties on it. Cook for about 7 minutes per side or until the beef is well cooked. Carefully remove the toothpick, place the patties in the buns and serve immediately.

Did you know?

Bacon contains a large amount of Choline, a compound that aids in the brain development in fetuses. The 3rd September is International Bacon Day.

41. Grilled Zesty Tilapia with a Sweet and Spicy Mango Salsa

Do not let the exhaustive list of ingredients intimidate you, this dish is extremely easy to prepare! If you do not like mangoes or cannot find them in your local market, you can substitute the mango for strawberries!

Ingredients

- 2/3 cup extra virgin olive oil
- 2 tablespoons lemon juice
- 2 tablespoons fresh parsley, minced
- 2 cloves garlic, minced
- 2 teaspoons dried basil
- 2 teaspoons ground black pepper
- 1 teaspoon salt
- 4 (6 ounce) tilapia fillets

For the Mango Salsa

- 2 large ripe mangos, peeled, pit removed and diced
- 1 red bell pepper, diced
- 1/4 cup red onion, minced
- 2 tablespoons fresh cilantro, chopped
- 2 jalapeno peppers, seeded and minced
- 1/4 cup lime juice
- 2 tablespoons lemon juice
- Salt, to taste
- Pepper, to taste

Method

1. Combine the lemon juice, extra virgin olive oil, basil, garlic, salt and pepper in a bowl. Pour the prepared marinade in a re-sealable bag and add the tilapia fillets to the bag. Remove the excess air from the bag and seal it shut. Shake the bag up to coat the fillets with the marinade. Place the bag in the refrigerator for about 2 hours.

2. To prepare the mango salsa, place the chopped mango, red onion, red bell pepper, jalapeno peppers, and cilantro in a small bowl. Pour in the lemon juice and lime juice and mix well. Taste and season accordingly with salt and pepper. Pop into the refrigerator to chill.

3. Turn up your grill to medium high heat and let it preheat for a few minutes. Lightly spray the grate with some cooking spray. Carefully remove the tilapia fillets from the marinade and lightly dab with an absorbent towel to get rid of the excess marinade.

4. Place the fillets on the preheated and prepared grill and grill for about 4 minutes per side or until the fish gets opaque in the center and easily flakes when flaked with a fork.

5. To serve, place the grilled tilapia on a plate and spoon a healthy helping of the prepared mango salsa on the fillet. Serve immediately.

Did you know?

The mango is known as the "king of fruits" and is a rich source of vitamin A, vitamin B6, Vitamin C, vitamin E and copper.

42. Orange and Garlic Grilled Tuna

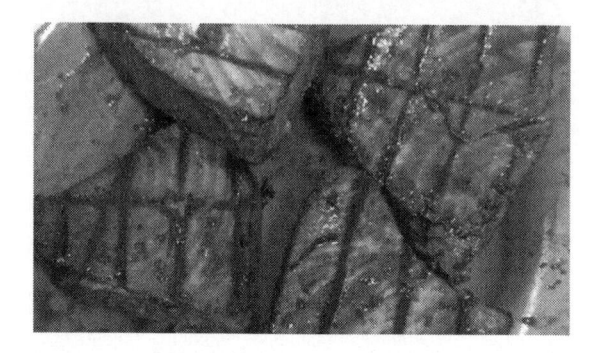

The tangy and savory combination of orange juice and garlic gives this dish a delicious and strong flavor.

Ingredients

- 1/2 cup orange juice
- 1/4 cup fresh parsley, chopped
- 1/2 cup soy sauce
- 2 tablespoons lemon juice
- 1/4 cup olive oil
- 1 teaspoon fresh oregano, chopped
- 2 cloves garlic, minced
- 1 teaspoon ground black pepper
- 8 (4 ounce) tuna steaks

Method

1. Combine the orange juice, olive oil, soy sauce, garlic, lemon juice, parsley, pepper and oregano in a large glass dish. Put the tuna steaks in the prepared marinade and flip over and over to coat well. Place the dish with the marinade and steaks in the refrigerator for about 30 minutes.

2. Turn up the grill to high heat and preheat. Lightly grease the grate with some oil. Place the marinated tuna steaks on the grill and keep the extra marinade. Cook the steak for about 5 minutes on one side, flip over, baste with the marinade and keep cooking until done. Serve hot!

Did you know?

Tuna is rich in protein, omega 3 fatty acids, vitamin D and Selenium. Selenium is a rarely found nutrient that plays an important role in boosting the immune system of the body.

43. Sweet Pineapple Chicken Skewers

This recipe is ideal for the days when you want to have a light meal without heavy meats weighing you down.

Ingredients

- 4 pounds chicken breast or strips, cut into bite sized pieces
- 2 cups pineapple juice
- 2/3 cup light soy sauce
- 1 cup packed brown sugar
- Skewers

Method

1. Soak the skewers in some warm water for about 20 minutes. Drain and dry on an absorbent towel. Heat a small saucepan over a medium flame. Pour in the pineapple juice and let it heat through for a minute. Add in the soy sauce and brown sugar and mix well. Take the mixture of heat just before it starts boiling.

2. Put the chicken pieces in a medium sized bowl. Pour the pineapple mix over the chicken, completely covering the chicken. Cover the bowl using a plastic wrap and refrigerate for about 30 minutes, or more if possible.

3. Turn up your grill to medium low heat and grease the grate with some oil or cooking spray. Skewer the marinated chicken pieces on the prepared skewers.

4. Place the chicken skewers on the prepared and preheated grill and cook for about 7 minutes per side or until the chicken is done. Watch the skewers closely, as the pineapple juice caramelizes quickly, resulting in easy burning. Serve hot!

Did you know?

Soy sauce is considered to be one of the oldest condiments of the world, and has been used to prepare dishes in China since almost 2,500 years now.

44. Country-Style Pork Ribs

What would a barbeque be without some finger-licking good pork ribs?

Ingredients

- 3 1/2 pounds country-style pork ribs
- 2 tablespoons salt
- 2 tablespoons golden brown sugar
- 2 teaspoons chili powder
- 1/2 teaspoon cumin powder
- 2 teaspoons chipotle seasoning
- 1/2 teaspoon garlic powder
- 1/2 teaspoon onion powder

Method

1. Mix together everything but the pork well so that it is completely combined. Rub evenly all over the ribs. Put the ribs, covered, in the refrigerator and leave them to marinate for a minimum of 7-8 hours. If possible, leave them overnight for the best flavor.

2. Take them out of the refrigerator around about an hour before you want to start grilling them so that they can come down to room temperature. You will need to grill them over a medium heat.

3. Oil the grill and then place the ribs onto it. If you have a cover, use it now. Let the ribs grill for around 6 or 7 minutes on each side or

so that the pork browns and a nice crust forms. You also want to do the bottom side of the ribs the same way. To help them stand up, you may need to form a tepee shape with them. Take off the grill and let it rest under cover for about 5 minutes or so before cutting it up.

Did you know?

The particular cut chosen here may look like rib meat, but it isn't. It is actually boneless and are cut quite close to the pig's shoulder. You can use this same recipe and slow-roast them in the oven if you like. You'll know they are done when the meat develops a nice crust but is fork-tender.

45. Simple and Tender Prime Rib

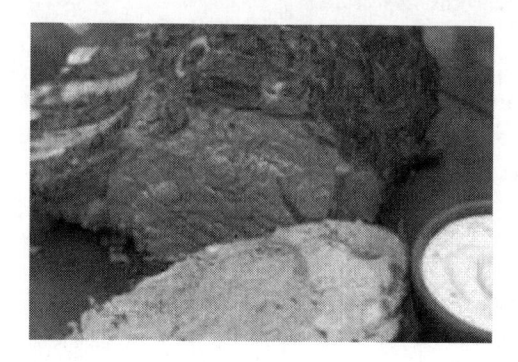

Prime rib is one of the most flavorsome cuts of meat. It has the perfect blend of fat and meat.

Ingredients

- An 8-pound beef rib roast
- 2 tablespoons salt
- 2 tablespoons olive oil
- 1 1/2 teaspoons freshly ground black pepper
- Horseradish Sauce (Optional)

Method

1. Place a wire rack onto a baking sheet and place the roast on top of this. Cover it with some paper towel and place in the refrigerator. Allow the surface of the meat to dry completely.

2. Take the roast out of the refrigerator around about an hour before you want to start cooking it. Mix together oil, salt and pepper and rub all over the meat. Set aside for at least an hour to allow the meat to absorb the flavor.

3. In the meanwhile, you can start to get the grill fired up. You need to use a drip pan when using charcoal for this recipe so that the fire doesn't flame when the fat drips off it.

4. Allow the charcoal to get flaming hot and move the coals to one side carefully. Put the drip tray next to the coals. Place the grill back on and cook the roast over the drip tray. Cook the meat,

rotating every half an hour or so in order to let every side get some exposure to the hot coals.

5. You can check for doneness by using a meat thermometer. If placed in the thickest part of the meat, away from the bone, the reading should read 125°F for medium rare. This will take a couple of hours or so and you will have to keep an eye on the coals, topping them up as necessary. If you like your meat cooked more, allow it to cook for longer.

6. When done, place in a foil tent to allow the meat to rest. It needs to rest for about 10 minutes before you cut it. Serve with horseradish sauce.

Did you know?

Horseradish is not a difficult herb to grow so you can grow it to make your own sauce. However, care needs to be taken during harvesting and preparation because the flesh contains compounds that can irritate the skin.

46. Gourmet Steak with All the Fixings

Cheese, bacon and steak. Is there a more heavenly combination?

Ingredients

The Steak

- 1 pound of skirt steak, have it cut widthwise into three portions
- 3 crushed garlic cloves
- 1/2 cup red wine
- 2 teaspoons salt
- 1 tablespoon black pepper, powdered
- 4 skewers

The Topping

- ½ a mild onion, chopped into quarters, with layers separated out
- 1 ounce of crumbled blue cheese
- 8 ounces mushrooms, clean well and remove the stems
- Vegetable oil
- 4 rashers of bacon
- Salt and pepper to taste
- 2 teaspoons parsley, chopped up nice and finely
- 2 tablespoons Worcestershire sauce

Method

1. For the steak, put all the ingredients except for the steak in a dish large enough to lay the steak out in a single layer and stir well. Put

the steak in and flip to ensure all sides are coated. Place covered in the refrigerator for at least two hours. Flip the steak around about half-way through.

2. While waiting for the meat to marinade, you can get the vegetables ready. Place the mushrooms and onion onto the skewers. Don't worry about mixing them up, at this point we just want to get them cooked.

3. Brush both lots of veggies with some oil. For the mushrooms, follow this up with some Worchester sauce. Season the mushrooms and onions to taste and set them aside. Get your flat grill plate out and coat it with a thin layer of oil or non-stick cooking spray.

4. Cook the bacon until it is nice and crispy. Set it aside to cool and then crumble it up. You will cook the vegetables next. Baste the mushrooms with Worchester sauce every couple of minute and cook until the mushrooms are done and the onions start to caramelize, turning often. Set aside, covered with foil.

5. Now it's time for the steak. Take the steak out and pat dry using a paper towel. The leftover marinade can be thrown out. Grease the grill plates again and cook the steak until done to your liking. You should only flip the meat once during this time. For a medium-rare steak, this will take a little over five minutes from start to finish. Set aside to rest.

6. Now you can take the veggies off the skewers. Quarter the mushrooms and chop up the onions coarsely. Mix in with the bacon and then stir in the parsley and cheese. Season as required. Slice up the steak and top with the topping.

Did you know?

The mold used in the production of blue cheese is Penicillium.

47. BBQ Beef Ribs

This is a fiery recipe, so you have to be able to handle the heat. For those who love a bit of spice, though, this is as close to heavenly as you'll get.

Ingredients

The ribs

- 1/4 cup paprika
- 1 tablespoon chili powder
- 5 pounds beef short ribs (About two inches thick)
- 1 tablespoon ground cumin
- 1 tablespoon dark brown sugar
- 2 teaspoons cayenne pepper
- Salt and pepper to taste
- 1 teaspoon garlic powder

The sauce

- 1/4 cup mild onion, chopped up nice and finely
- 1 tablespoon vegetable oil
- 3 crushed garlic cloves
- 1/2 cup packed dark brown sugar
- 1 1/2 cups ketchup
- 2 chipotles, finely chopped
- 1/2 cup water
- 3 tablespoons Worcestershire sauce
- 3 tablespoons apple cider or white wine vinegar

Method

1. For the sauce, set your stove to medium and warm up the oil in a medium-sized pot. Stir the garlic and onion in and cook until they start to soften.

2. Whisk in the rest of the ingredients and heat, stirring all the while, until the start to boil. Put the heat on low and cook for half an hour, or until the sauce is thick and sticky. Remove and set aside.

3. For the ribs, mix everything but the ribs together and make sure the mixture is completely mixed. Lay out the ribs in an oven-proof dish that is large enough to accommodate them in one layer. Rub the ribs with the spices so that they are evenly coated. Place the dish covered in the refrigerator and leave overnight for the flavors to develop.

4. Remove them from the refrigerator at least an hour before you need to cook them. You will need to pre-cook them so cook them until just done in the oven or on the grill the day before you need them.

5. Fire up the grill until you have got a medium heat going. Brush the sauce onto the ribs and then lay them onto the grill. Shut the lid and let the ribs cook for around about 5 minutes or so. Turn the ribs over and baste with the sauce again. Cook for a further 5 minutes, flip and baste again. Repeat twice more so that the ribs are warm throughout and the sauce has thickened to a glaze on the ribs. Warm up the leftover sauce and use as a dipping sauce.

Did you know?

Pork is the most widely eaten meat worldwide.

48. Steak Sandwich

This is a great recipe to use for leftover steak.

Ingredients

- 3 to 4 ounces flank steak, sliced
- 2 tablespoons mayo
- 1 1/2 ounces cheese, sliced nice and thinly
- 2 tablespoons of bell peppers, sliced finely
- A 3-inch long slice of ciabatta, sliced in half horizontally

Method

1. Place your broiler on high and put the rack in the center of your oven. Place the slices of ciabatta on a baking sheet. Divide the mayo evenly between the two slices. Put the cheese onto one piece of ciabatta and the peppers and steak in layers on the other.

2. Place in the oven and cook until the cheese has started to melt. This will take about three or four minutes so watch it carefully, so it doesn't burn.

Did you know?

Ciabatta is the Italian answer to the French baguette. The recipe is only about 35 years old.

49. Rib Steaks with a Fresh Salad

The beans make a great tasting alternative to boring lettuce in this tasty salad.

Ingredients

For the steak

- 2 teaspoons garlic powder
- 2 teaspoons ground mustard
- 3 pounds of thick cut rib steaks
- Salt and pepper to taste

For the salad

- 2 tablespoons shallot, chopped up nice and finely
- 2 teaspoons lemon zest

For the Salad

- 6 tablespoons lemon juice, fresh is best
- Salt and pepper to taste
- 2 pounds green beans, topped and tailed
- 1/2 cup parsley, freshly picked and chopped
- 1/2 cup good quality olive oil
- 1 pound of cherry or Rosa tomatoes, halved

Method

1. For the steak, mix together the seasoning, garlic and mustard well. Use the mixture to evenly coat the steak. Set aside, covered, at room temperature, for around an hour. The rub needs to be absorbed.

2. Fire up the grill so that the heat is high. Lay out the steaks on the grill and cook until done to your liking, flipping only once. For a medium rare steak, this will normally take about 10 minutes in total. You'll know that the steak is done when it feels firmer when you press down on it or when a meat thermometer inserted into the thickest part of the meat reads 130°F. Allow the steak to rest for around 5 or 10 minutes before you start to cut them.

3. For the salad, take a large pot and fill up to a quarter full of ice. Add enough water to fill the pot halfway and put to one side.

4. Using a second pot that will fit into the first, bring a pot of water to the boil and salt. Cook the green-beans for a few minutes until they are just done but stull crunchy. Drain out the boiling water and put the pot with the beans in it into the ice bath to stop them cooking any further.

5. Now mix together the zest, lemon juice and shallot together. Whisk in the oil a little at a time and put to one side. Put the parsley, tomatoes and beans into a salad bowl and coat with the dressing. Adjust the seasoning if necessary.

Did you know?

The shallot is a type of onion but is milder than your standard onion.

50. Olive and Cheese Burger

This is yet another burger – no, we can't get enough of them either. This time, however, the burger has a gourmet twist.

Ingredients

- 2 tablespoons good quality olive oil
- 2 pounds ground, low-fat chuck
- 4 ounces of Monterey Jack
- About 1/2 cup Tapenade
- Salt and pepper to taste
- 4 slices of ciabatta
- 1 tomato, sliced as thinly as possible
- Lettuce

Method

1. Make four evenly sized patties from the meat. (Make them smaller and thicker if you prefer your burgers medium-rare.) If need be, make them up to two days ahead of time and refrigerate them in a covered container until needed. Season to taste.

2. Heat the grill until it is at a medium high heat. Place the burgers on the grill, for around 8-10 minutes per side or until done to your liking. You should resist the urge to press the patties down during this time as it can make the meat tougher.

3. About a minute or so before you are ready to take the burgers off, place some of the cheese on top so that it can melt. Take the

burgers off the grill and keep them warm so that they can rest for about 5 minutes before they are served.

4. In the meantime, get the buns ready by buttering them and spreading the tapenade on top. Layer the lettuce and tomato on top, add the burger and then finish off with some more tapenade. Serve straight away.

Did you know?

Tapenade is traditionally made from a mixture of olives, capers and olive oil, finely chopped up.

51. Sweet and Sour Grilled Steak and Peppers

Ingredients

For the steak

- 3/4 cup olive oil
- 2 pounds of flank steak, cleaned and extra fat trimmed off
- 1 tablespoon water
- 1/3 cup balsamic vinegar
- 1 crushed garlic clove
- 1 1/2 teaspoons marjoram, freshly picked and chopped
- 2 teaspoons dark brown sugar
- Salt and pepper to taste

For the relish

- 1/4 cup coarsely chopped, pitted green olives
- 2 yellow bell peppers
- 1 red bell pepper
- Salt and pepper to taste

Method

1. For the relish, put the whole peppers onto your grill. If you have a cover, close it and let the peppers cook until they start to blister and go black. You'll need to turn them once or twice during the cooking time. Overall, it should be about 25 minutes.

2. Put the peppers into a big bowl and immediately cover the bowl with cling wrap or a plate, so that the peppers can sweat. Set aside to cool.

3. Take the peppers out of the bowl, and reserve the liquid in the bowl. The skins of the peppers should be easy to remove. Just scrape them off and then deseed and chop the peppers up. Put them back in the bowl and stir in the reserved marinade. Adjust the seasoning as necessary and serve with the steak.

4. For the steak, season the steak to your taste and then blend together the remaining ingredients to make a marinade. Reserve about three tablespoons of it to use in the relish. Place the steak in a baking dish and coat with the marinade. Flip the pieces so that every side is coated and then set it aside covered for about fifteen minutes. Flip the steak and leave for another 15 minutes.

5. Set your grill to a high heat. Take the steak out of the marinade, allowing any extra marinade to drain off. Cook the steak on the grill, turning only once. For a medium-rare steak, this will take about 10 minutes in total. Alternatively, the steak is done when a meat thermometer inserted into the thickest part reads about 130°F.

6. Take the steak off the grill and place it in a foil tent so that it can rest. It should be allowed to rest for at least 10 minutes before it is cut.

Did you know?

To cook your steak perfectly, you must wait until the grill is nice and hot before putting the steaks on it.

52. Quesadillas with a Difference

A new take on the tortilla for your next South of the Border themed party.

Ingredients

- 1 pound of skirt steak, sliced
- Salt and black pepper to taste
- 1 chipotle, finely chopped
- 16 ounces cheese, shredded
- 1/3 cup jalapeños pickle
- 8 large tortillas

Method

1. Fire up the grill until it is hot. Take your steak and, using paper towels, dry the outside of it. Brush on the chipotle and season to taste.

2. Cook the steak on the grill, turning only once. For a medium-rare steak, this will take about 10 minutes in total. Alternatively, the steak is done when a meat thermometer inserted into the thickest part reads about 130°F.

3. Let the steak rest for about five minutes and then cut into bite-sized pieces. Take the quesadillas over to the grill and cook until the tortillas crisp up and the cheese melts, turning halfway through the cooking time. Slice the quesadillas and serve hot with guacamole, sour cream and salsa to taste.

Did you know?

The younger a jalapeño pepper is, the milder it normally is. As the pepper matures, it turns red – the redder the color, the hotter it should be.

53. Japanese-Style Grill

Add some Japanese flavor to your next barbeque with this tasty recipe.

Ingredients

- 5 medium garlic cloves, minced
- 6 tablespoons red miso
- 2 tablespoons mirin
- 2 tablespoons sugar
- 2 tablespoons sake
- 2 pounds skirt steak, cut into strips
- 1 tablespoon tobanjan

Method

1. Mix the sugar, sake, tobanjan, mirin, garlic and miso together and stir until the sugar completely dissolves. Lay out the steak in an oven dish large enough to accommodate it in a single layer and pour the marinade over it. Flip the steak to make sure that it is completely coated. Let it sit in the marinade at room temperature for about an hour.

2. Fire up the grill until a medium high heat is reached. Cook the steak on the grill, turning only once. For a medium-rare steak, this will take about 10 minutes in total. Alternatively, the steak is done when a meat thermometer inserted into the thickest part reads about 130°F. Remove it and set it aside to rest for around about 10 minutes or so.

Did you know?

Miso is from Japan and is made from fermented barley, soy or rice. Miso comes in two basic varieties – Shiro, white miso that tastes sweet and mild or aka, red miso that has been allowed to age and has a more salty, savory taste. Miso is normally stored in the refrigerator.

Conclusion

Well, that's about it. I hope that you have found these recipes interesting and that you are all fired up to get your grill all fired up. As I always say when it comes to good cooking – the proof is in the flavor.

And one thing that these recipes all have in common is that they have lots of flavor.

Experiment with the recipes, get to know the basics of using your grill and, when you are ready, start coming up with your own great variations of these recipes.

At the end of the day, the best advice that I can give when it comes to being a master griller is to get out there and practice, practice, practice.

At the very least, you'll have a fun and very tasty journey.

On your marks, get set, and get grilling!

Final Words

I would like to thank you for downloading my book and I hope I have been able to help you and educate you about something new.

If you have enjoyed this book and would like to share your positive thoughts, could you please take 30 seconds of your time to go back and give me a review on my Amazon book page!

I greatly appreciate seeing these reviews because it helps me share my hard work!

Again, thank you and I wish you all the best with your cooking journey!

Last Chance to Get YOUR Bonus!

FOR A LIMITED TIME ONLY – Get Olivia's best-selling book *"The #1 Cookbook: Over 170+ of the Most Popular Recipes Across 7 Different Cuisines!"* absolutely FREE!

Readers have absolutely loved this book because of the wide variety of recipes. It is highly recommended you check these recipes out and see what you can add to your home menu!

Once again, as a big thank-you for downloading this book, I'd like to offer it to you *100% FREE for a LIMITED TIME ONLY!*

Get your free copy at:

TheMenuAtHome.com/Bonus

Disclaimer

This book and related site provides recipe and food advice in an informative and educational manner only, with information that is general in nature and that is not specific to you, the reader. The contents of this book and related site are intended to assist you and other readers in your personal efforts. Consult your physician or nutritionist regarding the applicability of any information provided in our information to you.

Nothing in this book should be construed as personal advice or diagnosis, and must not be used in this manner. The information provided about conditions is general in nature. This information does not cover all possible uses, actions, precautions, side-effects, or interactions of medicines, or medical procedures. The information in this site should not be considered as complete and does not cover all diseases, ailments, physical conditions, or their treatment.

No Warranties: The authors and publishers don't guarantee or warrant the quality, accuracy, completeness, timeliness, appropriateness or suitability of the information in this book, or of any product or services referenced by this site.

The information in this site is provided on an "as is" basis and the authors and publishers make no representations or warranties of any kind with respect to this information. This site may contain inaccuracies, typographical errors, or other errors.

Liability Disclaimer: The publishers, authors, and other parties involved in the creation, production, provision of information, or delivery of this site specifically disclaim any responsibility, and shall not be held liable for any damages, claims, injuries, losses, liabilities, costs, or obligations including any direct, indirect, special, incidental, or consequences damages (collectively known as "Damages") whatsoever and howsoever caused, arising out of, or in connection with the use or misuse of the site and the information contained within it, whether such Damages arise in contract, tort, negligence, equity, statute law, or by way of other legal theory.

Made in the USA
Middletown, DE
13 July 2019